CANTATE, ARIETE A UNA, DUE, E TRE VOCI

RECENT RESEARCHES IN THE MUSIC OF THE BAROQUE ERA

Christoph Wolff, general editor

A-R Editions, Inc., publishes seven series of musicological editions
that present music brought to light in the course of current research:

Recent Researches in the Music of the Middle Ages and Early Renaissance
Charles M. Atkinson, general editor

Recent Researches in the Music of the Renaissance
James Haar, general editor

Recent Researches in the Music of the Baroque Era
Christoph Wolff, general editor

Recent Researches in the Music of the Classical Era
Eugene K. Wolf, general editor

Recent Researches in the Music of the Nineteenth and Early Twentieth Centuries
Rufus Hallmark, general editor

Recent Researches in American Music
John M. Graziano, general editor

Recent Researches in the Oral Traditions of Music
Philip V. Bohlman, general editor

Each *Recent Researches* edition is devoted to works
by a single composer or to a single genre of composition.
The contents are chosen for their potential interest to scholars
and performers, then prepared for publication according to the
standards that govern the making of all reliable historical editions.

Subscribers to any of these series, as well as patrons of subscribing institutions,
are invited to apply for information about the "Copyright-Sharing Policy"
of A-R Editions, Inc., under which policy any part of an edition
may be reproduced free of charge for study or performance.

For information contact

A-R EDITIONS, INC.
801 Deming Way
Madison, Wisconsin 53717

(800) 736-0070 (U.S. book orders)
(608) 836-9000 (phone)
(608) 831-8200 (fax)
http://www.areditions.com

RECENT RESEARCHES IN THE MUSIC OF THE BAROQUE ERA • VOLUME 83

Barbara Strozzi

CANTATE, ARIETE A UNA, DUE, E TRE VOCI

OPUS 3

Edited by Gail Archer

A-R Editions, Inc.
Madison

ISBN 0-89579-388-1
ISSN 0484-0828

∞ The paper used in this publication meets the minimum requirements of the American National Standard for Information Sciences—Permanence of Paper for Printed Library Materials, ANSI Z39.48-1984.

Contents

Acknowledgments

Encouragement in both the choice of composer and place of compositional activity was enthusiastically provided by David Noon, whose devotion to the history and musical life of the Serene Republic is an inspiration. His guidance and assistance at the dissertation stage of my work was much appreciated. Further critical advice was offered by Jeffrey Langford, Arthur Lawrence, and George Stauffer, while Elizabeth Davis at the Columbia University music library offered her expertise as research progressed. Andy Brick's patience with me in acquiring the technological skills to complete the transcription is gratefully acknowledged.

This volume is dedicated to my son, Nicholas, whose example of strength and courage this year has inspired all who know and love him.

Introduction

Barbara Strozzi, a unique, feminine figure in a compositional field dominated by such contemporaries as Giacomo Carissimi, Luigi Rossi, Marc' Antonio Cesti, and Mario Savioni, stands out for the high quality and number of her vocal publications: seven volumes of secular works and one of sacred music. Compared with Carissimi and Rossi, who published about three percent of their output, Strozzi supervised the publication of just over one hundred works herself, more than any other seventeenth-century composer.[1] Further, she occupied a singularly fortunate social position as the adopted (and very likely illegitimate) daughter of the distinguished Venetian playwright and poet Giulio Strozzi (1583–1652). His intellectual milieu was the Accademia degli Incogniti, a group of philosophers, poets, historians, and clergy who published widely and were a major political and cultural force in Venice. Its members furnished librettos to all of the important Venetian opera composers and were responsible for the founding of the Teatro Novissimo (1641–45).[2] A subgroup of the Incogniti, the Accademia degli Unisoni, was established in 1637 in Strozzi's home specifically as a platform for Barbara's performances of her own works. Her skill as a lutenist and singer is reported in *Le veglie de' Signore Unisoni* (1638), a publication documenting both the musical activities and rhetorical debates of the society in which Barbara clearly took part.[3]

While most of the detailed scholarship concerning Strozzi's life has been done in the past twenty years, notably by Ellen Rosand, the composer was recognized as an important contributor and even originator of the cantata form in Italy as early as Charles Burney's *A General History of Music* (1789).

> The first time, however, that I have found the term CANTATA used for a short narrative lyric poem was in the *Musiche varie a voce sola del Signor Benedetto Ferrari da Reggio*, printed in Venice; which is twenty years more early than the period at which the invention of cantatas is fixed by some writers, who have given the honor to BARBARA STROZZI, a Venetian lady, who, in 1653, published vocal compositions under the title of CANTATE, *Ariette e Duetti*.[4]

Burney's remarks are significant in pointing directly to Strozzi's widespread fame as a musician, in underscoring his personal knowledge of opus 3 and its companion opus 2, which had already been cataloged in the British Library at the time Burney wrote,[5] and in mentioning Benedetto Ferrari, who with Francesco Manelli established public opera in Venice at the Teatro San Cassiano in 1637.

The first use of the term *cantade* appears in Alessandro Grandi's *Cantade et arie a voce sola*, reprinted in 1620 from an earlier source whose date is unknown.[6] From 1620–40 the cantata was a medium for experimentation and was known by many generic labels, including *arie, musiche, lamenti, madrigali, scherzi,* and *concerti*. These multiple terms actually describe a specific type of seventeenth-century music: a work for one to three voices composed of several sections in various styles and accompanied by basso continuo.[7] During these years Giovanni Pietro Berti, Francesco Turini, Domenico Crivellati, Giovanni Rovetta, Giovanni Felice Sances, and Benedetto Ferrari were among composers who describe their works as cantatas.[8] Monteverdi's late volumes of concerted madrigals, book 7, *Concerti* (1619), and book 8, *Madrigali guerreri et amorosi* (1624), published after his arrival in Venice in 1613, explore a wide range of vocal and instrumental combinations all anchored by the basso continuo.[9]

Unlike her male contemporaries, Barbara Strozzi's opportunities for employment and performance were narrowly restricted. It is not surprising then that she composed exclusively in the intimate genre of the cantata and that her first artistic collaborator was her father, Giulio Strozzi, who supplied the texts for opus 1 (1664). By the time of the second publication in 1651, only two of the twenty-six texts are attributed to the aging poet, who died the following year.[10] Among the sixteen other poets cited by Barbara, five (Giuseppe Artali, Nicolò Beregan, Pietro Paolo Bissari, Aurelio Aureli, and Giacinto Andrea Cicognini) also contributed libretti to the Venetian theaters.[11]

Opus 3 (1654) contains eleven cantatas: six solo cantatas for soprano, one duet for soprano and bass, two duets for soprano and alto, and two trios for soprano, alto, and bass. All include basso continuo. The texts may have been written by the founder of the Incogniti, Giovanni Francesco Loredano.[12] The poetry manifests a striking unity of expression in describing the pain, torment, and ephemeral nature of love. The sensuous, elegant, and yet artificial sentiments of the lyrics are born out in repeated references to love as a silent fire consuming the heart or fire as a chain dissolving a woman's beauty in a brief time span. According to the text of the seventh cantata, *Donna non sà che dice, non dice che sà,* women themselves are to blame, since they are inconsistent liars, unworthy of trust.

Unlike the distinguished poetry of the late sixteenth-century madrigal by such writers as Petrarch, Giambattista Guarini, Torquato Tasso, and Ariosto, seventeenth-century texts were intended for musical setting from the outset. The poetry of Gabriello Chiabrera (1522–1638) and in particular Giovanni Battista Marino (1569–1625) was favored by the cantata composers. The latter's "talent shone the brighter merely because he happened to live during the first years of that vast sequence of

Italian poetry . . . whose practitioners . . . have usually given themselves over to bombast, false heroics, sentimentality, and insipid persiflage."[13] Significantly, in 1633, Loredano wrote one of the earliest biographies of Marino.[14]

Another distinguishing feature of Strozzi's opus 3 is the absence of a written dedication. Instead, the motto *Ignotae Deae* appears above the figure of a veiled woman, an obvious reference to the Incogniti, who adopted this symbol as their logo. While the academicians use the masculine form, *Ignoto Deo,* Strozzi artfully alludes to her femininity and perhaps to the well-documented interest of the Incogniti in the cause of feminism.[15]

The Composer

Barbara Strozzi was born in Venice in 1619,[16] the daughter of Isabella Griega, also referred to as Isabella Garzone, "la Greghetta," a housemaid of Giulio Strozzi and heiress of his estate in a will of 1628. In a later testament (1650), the young girl of the household, previously referred to as Barbara Valle, is called "Barbara di Santa Sofia mia figliola elettiva però chiamata comunamente la Strozzi" (Barbara of Santa Sofia [the church in which she was baptized, 6 August 1619], my adopted daughter who is usually surnamed Strozzi). It has been suggested by Rosand that Giulio's use of the term *elletiva* refers both to Strozzi's legal adoption and probable illegitimacy.[17]

Strozzi's thorough grounding in arts and letters was assured by the influence of her prominent father, but there may have been another factor—education at one of the Venetian *ospedale*. The *ospedale* were charitable institutions established by the state to care for and educate the indigent and illegitimate who besieged Venice from the earliest times. Charity as practiced by monastic orders such as the Chevalier Hospitaliers de l'Order de Saint Lazare de Jerusalem, who founded the first of these institutions, the Mendicanti, during the twelfth century, was considered a means of insuring the eternal salvation of one's soul.[18]

Music was an important component of the educational program, especially at the Ospedale della Pietà, where orphan girls as young as three could be selected for membership in the *coro,* the performing vocal and instrumental ensembles.[19] In addition to the foundling girls or *figlia di coro,* there were also *figlia di spese,* daughters of the aristocracy and merchant classes, both foreign and domestic, who were accepted as paying boarders for a period of up to two years. The conservatory for boarders was established within the structure of the Pietà by the middle of the sixteenth century, and it is as a *figlia di spese* that Strozzi may have received her early musical instruction.[20]

Sometime before the publication of her opus 2 in 1651, Strozzi also studied with composer and organist Francesco Cavalli through the good offices of her father, whose intention clearly was to elevate her technical accomplishment to the professional level. In her preface to opus 2, the composer acknowledges that *"Francesco Cavalli . . . [era] già dalla mia fanciulezza mio cortese precettore"* (Francesco Cavalli . . . was already from my youth my courteous preceptor).[21] Cavalli, with forty-two operas to his credit, was closely associated with Monteverdi during the latter's tenure as maestro di cappella at San Marco in the first half of the seventeenth century. Cavalli served as second organist from 1640, as first organist from January 1665, and finally as maestro in his own right, in 1668.[22] Whether he engaged in formal studies with Monteverdi is unknown.[23]

The key difference between Barbara and her mentor and other male contemporaries is their ability to hold the major musical posts in churches, courts, and theaters and her inability to secure any professional employment whatsoever. To this end the composer deliberately chose her dedicatees from the highest ranks of the nobility, among them Ferdinand III of Austria, Anne of Austria, Francesco Carafa (prince of Belvedere), Doge Nicolò Sagredo, and Vittoria della Rovere, the grand duchess of Tuscany. The dedication of the first volume of cantatas, opus 1 (1664), to the Florentine duchess casts light on her unsuccessful efforts to obtain patronage:

> I must reverently consecrate this first work, which as a woman I publish all too boldly, to the Most August Name of Your Highness so that, under an oak of gold it may rest secure against the lightning bolts of slander prepared for it.[24]

While the obsequious style of her sentiments is typical, the final phrase brings up the critical issue of a woman's appropriate role in seventeenth-century society. Women who took part in theatrical or musical activities were often regarded as persons of questionable virtue, there being a link between music making and the numerous courtesans for which Venice was famous. In 1588 Pope Sixtus V banned the appearance of women in public theaters in Rome and in the Papal States.[25] In the succeeding century, on 4 May 1686, Pope Innocent XI declared "music is completely injurious to the modesty that is proper for the [female] sex because they become distracted from the matters and occupations most proper to them."[26] Further damaging criticism of women in music is stated by Pietro Aretino: "the knowledge of playing musical instruments, of singing, and of writing poetry on the part of women is the very key which opens the gates of their modesty."[27] Barbara Strozzi, as the acknowledged raison d'être of the Accademia degli Unisoni, is the object of slander in an anonymous manuscript, *Satire, et altre raccolte per l'Academie de gl 'Unisoni in casa di Giulio Strozzi:* the collection alludes to her granting sexual favors to members of the group and even to a liaison with a castrato, thus explaining away her infertility.[28]

Whether or not Barbara Strozzi was a skilled purveyor of the art of love, what is certain is that she moved and worked in the same circle of composers and literati as Monteverdi and Cavalli. The myriad influences of family, education, social, intellectual, and musical associates, and the liberal atmosphere of Venice itself made possible Barbara's distinguished career as a performing artist and composer.

The Music of the Edition

The eleven cantatas of *Cantate, ariete a una, due, e tre voci* may be considered in three groups: numbers 1–2, solo settings of strophic poetry that receive new musical settings for each verse, and number 3, an extended political lament; numbers 4–6, short, strophic cantatas; and the closing ensembles, the duets of numbers 7–9 and the trios of numbers 10 and 11.

The most striking feature of the two opening pieces is the sensitive, expressive handling of the text supported by frequently changing metric schemes. The anguish of the lover in the opening piece is rendered in brief ascending scale motifs that conclude in a flourish of sixteenth notes on "foco" using the entire D-minor scale (mm. 7–9). In the final twelve bars of the piece, descending chromatic steps depict the lover's own tongue as the agent of death (Terza parte, mm. 175–86). At the first change of tempo and meter (Prima parte, mm. 31–35), the composer highlights the lover's frustration by the use of recurring mottos of neighboring tones at each text repetition while "breaths and sighs" (mm. 49–51) are given both a visual and musical portrayal in pitches deftly separated by rests.

The pleasure the composer took in visual and musical images is evident at the outset of *Moralità amorosa* in the improvisatory freedom of the vocal line enhanced by the simplicity of the harmonic underlay (mm. 1–5) for the lyrical setting of the rising dawn. Chains of quarter notes in the Terza parte provide another example (mm. 91–109).

The third cantata of the print, *Il lamento*, is outstanding for its length, subject matter, and inclusion in both opus 2 and opus 3. The poem is an extended narrative concerning the misadventures of a French courtier, Henri di Cinq-Mars, who plotted unsuccessfully against Cardinal Richelieu and consequently forfeited the king's favor and his life. Ample precedent exists for this type of extended piece in Monteverdi's "Lament" from *Arianna*,[29] in similar political laments by Luigi Rossi and Giacomo Carissimi,[30] and in Cavalli's opera *L'Ormindo* (1644), which features a lament containing thirty-two repetitions of a passacaglia or ground bass figure meant to underline the solemnity of the hero's death.[31] The central portion of Strozzi's piece (mm. 100–139) also incorporates this technique.

Arguably the most attractive pieces are the three short ariettas at the center of the volume (nos. 4–6). Even when working on a small scale, the composer maintains a predilection for contrasting meter and tempo; the binary design of *A donna bella e crudele* juxtaposes the compound triple meter of the A section with the running eighth notes in $\frac{4}{4}$ of the B section. Similarly, the twelve bar refrain of *Amor non si fugge* effectively functions as the recurring element in a miniature rondo, ABABA, in which the alternate portions are in $\frac{4}{4}$ and $\frac{6}{4}$ meter.[32] The formal clarity of the ariettas underscores the direct appeal of their melodies.

Perhaps less successful are the ensemble pieces that round out the print. They reveal the same interest in metrical contrast as the earlier entries but are more diffuse in melodic invention. The B section of *Mentita*, a duet for soprano and mezzo soprano, for example, presents rather repetitious scale motifs that have little clear direction and limited range (mm. 33–43). The comic touches in the patter among the three pastoral characters Dori, Filindo, and Tirsi as they argue "si" or "no" in *Cor donato, cor rubato*, however, are rhythmically crisp and precise, as are the brief imitative germs of the duet *Begli occhi* (mm. 7–10).

In his *A General History of Music* (1789), Charles Burney remarks:

> Indeed, it is to be lamented that a species of composition so admirably calculated for concerts as the *cantata*, should be so seldom cultivated: as it contains a little drama entire, having a beginning, a middle, and an end in which the charms of poetry are united with those of Music, and the mind is amused while the ear is gratified.[33]

This edition is offered in the hope that these pieces will be performed by students and professionals alike in response to Burney's complaint and as a welcome addition to the seventeenth-century repertoire.

Notes on Performance

There are no indications in Gardano's 1654 print concerning the performing forces, nor is there a preface written by the composer that might shed light on a specific occasion when the cantatas of opus 3 were performed. The *Veglie de' Signore Unisoni* (1638) documents Strozzi's skill as both a lutenist and singer, which suggests that a private performance before members of the Accademia degli Unisoni was the likely venue. The fact that the texts were probably supplied by Giovanni Francesco Loredano, the founder of the larger academy, the Accademia degli Incogniti, supports this view. Strozzi's virtuosity as a singer is also affirmed by Nicolò Fontei's dedication in the second volume of his *Bizzarrie poetiche* (1635).[34]

Early seventeenth-century musicians such as Lodovico Viadana, Giovanni Piccioni, and Agostino Agazzari wrote detailed accounts of their practice when preparing performances of new music. Some of their guidelines are instructive to modern performers attempting to solve problems presented by early scores and intelligently reconstruct what may have been Strozzi's performance practice.

In the preface to his *Cento concerti ecclesiastici* (1602), Viadana asserts, "I have not failed to introduce, where appropriate, certain figures and cadences, and other convenient opportunities for ornaments and passagework and for giving other proofs of the aptitude and elegant style of the singers."[35] Compositional practice in the seventeenth century followed on a century of courtly performance practice that encouraged the singers to respond to the sense of the text. As early as 1528, Castiglione remarks that he enjoyed, "singing to a lute and reciting."[36] While many continuo parts for secular music were not published, early seventeenth-century operatic scores by Jacopo Peri, monodies by Giulio Caccini, and *sacre rappresentazione* by Emilio de' Cavalieri were. They include figures beneath the bass lines that permit the clear execution of chords on a variety of fundament instruments and, more importantly, take into consideration flexible interpretation of the melody by the singer.[37]

Barbara Strozzi's cantatas abound in composed ornamentation in the vocal lines while the bass lines are almost devoid of *sigma,* or flats and sharps, and *numeri,* or figures.[38] There is evidence that there was opposition to the use of figures in the continuo. Mario Savioni, in his *Concerti morali* (1660) and *Madrigali morali* (1668), omitted most of the figures because of "the confusion that would be made between the notes and the words."[39] An earlier treatise of 1610 by the Venetian Giovanni Piccioni agrees that figures "are confusing rather than otherwise, while to the knowledgeable and expert, such signs are unnecessary, for they play them correctly by ear and by art."[40]

The instrument of Strozzi's art was the lute, cited by Agazzari as "the noblest instrument of them all."[41] The light construction and stringing of the instrument produced a highly expressive, warm tone best suited to chamber performance. Classic technique required that the string be struck with the soft cushion of the fingers and thumb, but a refined technique was difficult to acquire due to the demands of awkward chord positions and the need to sustain pressure on the strings.[42]

Achieving the balance between accompaniment and vocal line required restraint, good taste, and a thorough grounding in the performance tradition and its rules in order that one might not "obscure the excellence of the note itself or of the passage which the good singer executes upon it."[43] The amount of affective ornamentation contained in Strozzi's melodies juxtaposed with an unfigured bass, which contemporary accounts confirm was the professional standard, suggests that very little ornamentation need be added to the cantatas, except at cadences, and that the composer's aim was clarity and simplicity of expression. In a few cantatas, Strozzi includes the sign "*t.*" to stand for the *trillo,* a vocal ornament performed by repercussions of the notated pitch.[44] This has been rendered in this edition as a modern trill sign (*tr*). The single instance of an instrumental ritornello is found in *Il lamento* and should be played entirely by the continuo.

Since tempo markings appear in three of the cantatas, an understanding of their meaning is of interest to the modern performer. Markings such as *adagio* and *presto* were often added to seventeenth-century scores to signal a change from the original tempo and then its restoration. In some scores these terms were associated respectively with the dynamic markings *piano* and *forte,* suggesting a terracing of both speed and volume.[45]

Purcell's edition of *Sonnata's of III Parts* (1683) declares, "Adagio and Grave . . . import nothing but a very slow movement,"[46] while Brossard's *Dictionaire de musique* (1703) states, "Presto means, Fast. That is to say the speed must be pressed on, by making the beats very short."[47] Considering the context in which Strozzi uses tempo indications, a straightforward contrast is implied in *Cuore che reprime alla lingua di manifestare il nome della sua cara* and *Begli occhi,* and a lively tempo is the intention for the second half of *A donna bella e crudele.*

Notes

1. Ellen Rosand, "The Voice of Barbara Strozzi," in *Women Making Music: The Western Art Tradition 1150–1950,* ed. Jane Bowers and Judith Tick (Urbana: University of Illinois Press, 1987), 176.

2. Ellen Rosand, *Opera in Seventeenth-Century Venice: The Creation of a Genre* (Berkeley and Los Angeles: University of California Press, 1991), 37.

3. Rosand, "Voice of Barbara Strozzi," 169.

4. Charles Burney, *A General History of Music* (1789; reprint, New York: Harcourt, Brace, 1935), 605.

5. Ibid.

6. Nigel Fortune, "Italian Secular Monody from 1600–1635: An Introductory Survey," *Musical Quarterly* 39 (1953): 189.

7. Claude V. Palisca, *Baroque Music* (Englewood Cliffs, N.J.: Prentice Hall, 1968), 114.

8. R. B. Morris, "A Study of the Italian Solo Cantata before 1750" (Ph.D. diss., Indiana University, 1955), 9.

9. For a discussion of the dissolution of the madrigal, see Alfred Einstein, *The Italian Madrigal,* 3 vols. (Princeton: Princeton University Press, 1949), 2:836–72.

10. Rosand, "Voice of Barbara Strozzi," 174.

11. Ellen Rosand, "Barbara Strozzi, *virtuosissima cantatrice:* The Composer's Voice," *Journal of the American Musicological Society* 31 (1978): 263.

12. Ibid.

13. Fortune, "Italian Secular Monody," 193.

14. Rosand, "Barbara Strozzi," 263.

15. Anthony Newcomb, "Courtesans, Muses, or Musicians? Professional Woman in Sixteenth-Century Italy," in *Women Making Music,* 99.

16. The date of death is unknown but is usually fixed shortly after the last publication, opus 8, in 1664; see Ellen Rosand, "Barbara Strozzi," 280.

17. Ibid., 242.

18. Jane L. Baldauf-Berdes, *Women Musicians of Venice: Musical Foundations 1525–1855* (New York: Oxford University Press, 1993), 45.

19. Ibid., 101.

20. Ibid., 237.

21. Rosand, "Barbara Strozzi," 257.

22. H. C. Robbins-Landon and John Julius Norwich, *Five Centuries of Music in Venice* (New York: Schirmer Books, 1991), 98.

23. *The New Grove Dictionary of Music and Musicians,* s.v. "Cavalli, Francesco," by Thomas Walker.

24. Rosand, "Voice of Barbara Strozzi," 174.

25. Jane Bowers, "The Emergence of Women Composers in Italy, 1566–1700," in *Women Making Music,* 135.

26. Ibid., 139.

27. Einstein, *Italian Madrigal,* 1:94.

28. Rosand, "Barbara Strozzi," 251.

29. Henri Prunières, "The Italian Cantata of the XVII Century," *Music and Letters* 7 (1926): 42.

30. Rosand, "Barbara Strozzi," 265–66.

31. H. C. Wolff, "Italian Opera from Later Monteverdi to Scarlatti," in *The New Oxford History of Music* (London: Oxford University Press, 1975), 5:19.

32. *The New Grove Dictionary of Music and Musicians,* s.v. "Strozzi, Barbara," by Carolyn Raney.

33. Burney, *General History,* 638.

34. *The New Grove Dictionary of Music and Musicians,* s.v. "Strozzi, Barbara," by Carolyn Raney.

35. Lodovico Grossi da Viadana, foreword to *Cento concerti ecclesiastici* (Venice, 1602; English translation in Oliver Strunk, *Source Readings in Music History* (New York: W. W. Norton, 1950), 420.

36. *The New Grove Dictionary of Music and Musicians,* s.v. "Continuo," by Peter Williams.

37. Ibid.

38. Robert Donington, *The Interpretation of Early Music* (London: Faber and Faber, 1979), 289.

39. ". . . la confusione che farebbero trà le notte, e le parole"; see Irving R. Eisley, "The Secular Cantatas of Mario Savioni (1608–1685)" (Ph.D. diss., University of California, Los Angeles, 1964), 44.

40. Donington, *Early Music,* 291.

41. Agostino Agazzari, *Del sonare sopra il basso* (Rome, 1607; facsimile, Milan: Bollettino Bibliografico Musicale, 1933; English trans. in Strunk, *Source Readings,* 428.

42. Donington, *Early Music,* 545.

43. Agazzari, in Strunk, *Source Reading,* 427.

44. See Frederick Neumann, *Ornamentation in Baroque and Post-Baroque Music* (Princeton: Princeton University Press, 1987), 288–89.

45. *The New Grove Dictionary of Music and Musicians,* s.v. "Tempo and expression marks," by David Fallows.

46. Donington, *Early Music,* 388.

47. Ibid.

Texts and Translations

Spelling, orthography and punctuation have been modernized. The translations were prepared with the assistance of Stefano Mengozzi.

1. Cuore che reprime alla lingua di manifestare il nome della sua cara

The Heart that Prevents the Tongue from Expressing the Beloved's Name

Prima parte

Ardo in tacito foco
Neppure m'e concesso
Dal geloso cor mio
Far palese a me stesso
Il nome di colei ch'e 'l mio desio,
Ma nel carcer del seno
Racchiuso tien l'ardore,
Carcerier di se stesso, il proprio core.
E appena sia contento
Con aliti e sospiri
Far palese alla lingua i suoi martiri.

Part 1

I burn in silent fire and my jealous heart does not even allow me to reveal the name of she who is my desire, but in the prison of my breast the heart—its own guardian—keeps the passion enclosed, and it contents itself to disclose to the tongue its sufferings with sighs and breaths.

Seconda parte

Se pur per mio ristoro
Con tributi di pianto
Mostrar voglio con fede
A quella ch'amo tanto
Che son d'amor le lagrime mercede,
Ecco 'l cor ch'essalando
Di più sospiri il vento,
Assorbe il pianto e quell'umor n'ha spento
E con mio duol m'addita
Che gl'occhi lagrimanti
Sono mutole lingue negli amanti.

Part 2

Even if, for my own consolation, with offerings of tears I want faithfully to show to she whom I adore that these tears are the recompense of love, the heart, exhaling sighs, absorbs the tears and extinguishes my cry, and to my pain it shows that these weeping eyes are the mute tongues of the lovers.

Terza parte

Qual sia l'aspro mio stato
Ridir nol ponno i venti,
Neppur le selve o l'onde
Udiro i miei lamenti,
Ma solo il duol entro al mio cor s'asconde
E quale in chiuso specchio
Disfassi pietra al foco,
Tal io m'incenerisco a poco a poco
E s'ad altri la lingua
É scorta alla lor sorte,
A me la lingua è sol cagion di morte.

Part 3

The winds cannot convey the bitterness of my state, and neither the woods nor the waves heard my laments. The pain alone enters and is hidden within my heart. So as a stone melts in the fire under a concave mirror, so I turn into ashes little by little; and if for others the tongue helps them to their destiny, for me the tongue is only a reason of death.

2. Moralità amorosa

Amorous Morality

Prima parte

Sorge il mio sol con mattutini albori
E intento a coltivar beltà divine,
Con profumi odorosi incensa il crine
Per aditar altrui come s'adori.

Part 1

My sun rises with the early dawning, busy cultivating divine beauties, with fragrant perfume incensing her hair to show to others how one should be adorned.

Seconda parte

Poscia con sottilissimi candori
Sparge dell' aureo capo ogni confine,
Che di polve di cipri argente e brine
Fanno officio di smalto in su quegli ori.

Terza parte

Mentre cosi la bella man s'impiega
E fra ceneri e fumi il crine involve,
In catene di foco il cor mi lega.

Quarta parte

Che meraviglia è poi se si dissolve
La bellezza in brev'ora e chi mi nega
Che fugace non sia, s'e fumo e polve!

3. Il lamento

Sul Rodano severo
Giace tronco infelice
Di Francia il gran scudiero,
E s'al corpo non lice
Tornar di ossequio pieno
All'amato Parigi,
Con la fredd'ombra almeno
Il dolente garzon segue Luigi.

Enrico il bel, quasi annebbiato sole,
Delle guancie vezzose
Cangiò le rose in pallide viole
E di funeste brine
Macchiò l'oro del crine.
Lividi gl'occhi son, la bocca langue,
E sul latte del sen diluvia il sangue.

"Oh Dio, per qual cagione"
Par che l'ombra gli dica,
"Sei frettoloso andato
A dichiarar un perfido, un fellone,
Quel servo a te si grato?
Mentre, Franzese Augusto,
Di meritar procuri il titolo di Giusto?
Tu, se 'l mio fallo di gastigo è degno,
Ohimè, ch'insieme insieme
Dell'invidia che freme
Vittima mi sacrifichi allo sdegno.

Non mi chiamo innocente:
Purtroppo errai, purtroppo
Ho me stesso tradito
A creder all' invito di fortuna ridente.
Non mi chiamo innocente:
Grand'aura di favori
Rea la memoria fece
Di così stolti errori,
Un nembo dell' obblio
Fu la cagion del precipizio mio
Ma che dic'io? Tu, Sire—ah, chi nol vede?—
Tu sol, credendo troppo alla mia fede,
M'hai fatto in regia corte
Bersaglio dell'invidia e reo di morte.

Part 2

Then with finest white powders she spreads her golden head to every border, thus of dust of silver powders and frost an enamel is made upon her head.

Part 3

While the expert hand is thus employed, and among ashes and fumes the hair is transformed, my heart is entwined in chains of fire.

Part 4

What marvel it is then that beauty dissolves in a brief hour and who can deny that it is fleeting, when it is but fumes and dust!

The Lament

By the austere Rhone the body of the great French warrior lays down; and if it is impossible for the body to return with full obsequies to its beloved Paris, with his cold shadow, at least Luigi follows the poor squire.

Enrico the beautiful, almost as pale as the fading sun, his rosy girlish cheeks changed to pallid violet and fatal frost stains his golden curls. His eyes are bruised, his mouth languishes, and on his milky white breast the blood flows.

"Oh God, for what cause," it seems that the shade tells him, "to go in haste to declare a perfidy, a traitor, who served you so gratefully, while as a French king, you are trying to win for yourself the title of Just One? You, if my mistake is worthy of punishment, alas, that together in fuming envy you sacrificed me to disdain. I don't call myself innocent: unfortunately, I erred; unfortunately, I betrayed myself by believing the invitation of smiling fortune.

"I don't call myself innocent: the grand aura of favors made my memory guilty of such foolish errors; a cloud of oblivion was the reason for my fall. But what do I say? You, Lord—ah, who does not see it?—only you, believing too much in my faithfulness, made me in the royal court a target of envy and guilty of death.

Mentre al devoto collo
Tu mi stendevi quel cortese braccio,
Allor mi davi il crollo,
Allor tu m'apprestavi il ferro e 'l laccio.
Quando meco godevi
Di trastullarti in sollazzevol gioco,
Allor l'esca accendevi
Di mine cortigiane al chiuso foco.
Quella palla volante
Che percoteva il tuo col braccio mio
Dovea pur dirmi, oh Dio,
Mia fortuna incostante.

Quando meco gioivi
Di seguir cervo fuggitivo, allora
L'animal innocente
Dai cani lacerato
Figurava il mio stato,
Esposto ai morsi di accanita gente.
Non condanno il mio re, no, d'altro errore
Che di soverchio amore.

Di cinque marche illustri
Notato era il mio nome,
Ma degli emoli miei l'insidie industri
Hanno di traditrice alla mia testa
Data la marca sesta.
Ha l'invidia voluto
Che, se colpevol sono,
Escluso dal perdono
Estinto ancora immantinente io cada;
Col mio sangue ha saputo
De' suoi trionfi imporporar la strada.
Nella grazia del mio re
Mentr'in su troppo men vo,
Di venir dietro al mio piè
La fortuna si stancò.
Onde ho provato, ahi lasso,
Come dal tutto al niente è un breve passo."

Luigi, a queste note
Di voce che perdon supplice chiede,
Timoroso si scuote
E del morto garzon la faccia vede.
Mentre il re col suo pianto
Delle sue frette il pentimento accenna
Tremò Parigi e torbidossi Senna.

"While extending your gracious arm about my faithful neck, at that very moment you caused my collapse, preparing the iron and the noose. While you enjoyed yourself in delightful games, at that same moment you ignited the tinder of the enclosed fires of courtly intrigue. That flying ball that struck your arm with mine should have told me, oh God, of my inconstant fortune.

"When you were enjoying yourself with me following the escaping deer, at that very moment the innocent animal torn to pieces by dogs represented my own position, exposed to the bites of ruthless people. I don't condemn my king, no, of any other fault than excessive love.

"My name was noted with five illustrious marks, but the skillful snares of my followers have placed upon my head a sixth brand of traitor. Envy has wanted me—if guilty, excluded from pardon, and immanent death—to fall once more; with my blood, it has stained the path of its triumph. While I had risen too high in the favor of my king, fortune was too tired to follow in my footsteps. Therefore I have proved that from everything to nothing is but a brief step."

Luigi is shaken by this tone of voice which is asking for suppliant forgiveness and sees the face of the dead squire. While the King with his tears showed repentance for his impatience, Paris trembled and the Seine became muddy.

4. A donna bella e crudele

Perle care e pregiate
Dall'ocean venute,
Perchè state
Frà due labbra che son mute?
Gite a bocca che risponda
O tornate in grembo all'onda.

Neve, tu che cadesti
Sovra un alpestre scoglio,
Perchè resti
In quel sen pieno d'orgoglio?
Trova un petto più gentile
O ritorna all'Alpe vile.

To a Woman Lovely and Cruel

Dear and precious pearls come from the sea, why are you between two lips that are mute? Go to a mouth that will answer or return to the lap of the wave.

Snow, you that falls upon an alpine reef, why rest in that breast full of pride? Find a more gentle heart or return to the desolate Alps.

Oro, che nobil vanto
Sei dell'Indico lido,
Perchè tanto
Orni il crine a volto infido?
Vanne a men severa fronte
O ritorna in seno al monte.

Sangue, che sulle rose
Ha Ciprigna versato,
Chi ti pose
Ostro bel su volto ingrato?
Corri a guancie più serene
O alla Dea torna in le vene.

Stelle, voi che negl'occhi
Splendete di costei,
Che vi tocchi
D'illustrare occhi si rei?
Gite a ciglia meno altere
O tornate all' alte sfere?

Gold, that noble pride of the Indian shore, why do you adorn the hair of a faithless countenance? Go to a brow less severe or return to the heart of the mountain.

Blood, that Ciprigna has poured on the roses, who placed your lovely pigment upon an ungrateful face? Run to cheeks more serene or return to the veins of the goddess.

Stars, you that shine within her eyes, why do you enlighten eyes so guilty? Go to lashes less haughty or return to the highest spheres.

5. Con male nuove, non si può cantare

Questa, questa è la nuova
Ch'io v'ho da dire amanti,
ch'amando non si trova
Altro che pene e pianti.
Ben il mio cor il prova
E volete ch'io canti.

Senta, senta chi brama
La canzonetta udire:
Non s'ama, no, non s'ama
Senza pena e martire.
A chi m'invita e chiama
Altro non ho che dire.

Deh, cantar non mi fate,
Che la canzon peggiora!
Quante bevande ingrate
Fugge chi s'innamora!
Ha poca caritate
Chi vuol ch'io canti ancora.

With Bad News, One Cannot Sing

This, this is the news I have to say to you lovers, that in loving one finds nothing other than pains and sighs. My heart proves it all too well and you want me to sing it.

Listen, listen you that are eager to hear the song: One does not love, no, without pains and suffering. To others who invite or call me I have nothing more to say.

Hey, don't make me sing since the song just gets worse! Those who love flee many an ungrateful drink! Those who want me to continue to sing have little pity on me.

6. Amor non si fugge

Cara filli, quella tu sei ch'adoro,
Per te sola, per te languisco e moro.

Ben vid' io ch'un guardo adesca
Ch'allettando il seno adugge,
Ma pur ardo e 'l cor si strugge
Che non fugge d'amor chi seco tresca.

Cara filli, quella tu sei ch'adoro,
Per te sola, per te languisco e moro.

S'e il languir colpo d'amore
Fuggirò s'amor m'assale,
Ma 'l fuggir, ohimè, che vale?
Non si scioglie dal piè laccio del core.

Cara filli, quella tu sei ch'adoro,
Per te sola, per te languisco e moro.

You Cannot Escape Love

Dear love, you are the one that I adore, for you alone, for you I languish and die.

I see well enough that one charming glance entices your heart, but for this, I burn and my heart is consumed. Those who plot these things do not escape from love.

Dear love, you are the one that I adore, for you alone, for you I languish and die.

If I escape the sorrowful dart of love, love itself will assail me; but escape, ah me, what worth? One cannot untie the heartstrings from one's feet.

Dear love, you are the one that I adore, for you alone, for you I languish and die.

7. Donna non sà che dice, non dice che sà

Lusinghiera d'amori
La vezzosa speranza
È un veleno dei cori.

Oh Dio, ch'io so
La femminile usanza,
Non è di donna mai
Promessa vera.
Così va, molto ha più
Chi nulla spera.

Cianciosetta ridente
Con piena cortesia
Ai miei preghi acconsente.

Oh Dio, ch'io so
La femminil bugia;
Non è di donna mai
Bocca verace.
Così va, parla più
Donna che tace.

Mentitrice d'affetti
Tutta piacevolezza
Si dimostra ai miei detti!

Oh Dio, ch'io so
La femminil vaghezza;
Non è di donna mai
Salda la fede.
Cosi' va, gode più
Chi meno il crede.

8. Mentita

S'io vi giuro mia vita
Ch'io v'amo
Voi mi date con parole spietate
Subito una mentita.

Io che sensi ho vivace
Corro l'affronto
À scaricar coi baci.

9. Begli occhi

Mi ferite, oh begli occhi.

Pensate che farebbono
Quei baci si cocenti e mordaci;
Langue l'anima, langue
E il cor vien meno.
Ahi ch'io vi moro in seno.

Pensate che farebbono
Gli strali si pungenti e mortali;
Langue l'anima, langue
E il cor vien meno.
Ahi ch'io vi moro in seno.

Ma forse non morò
Senza vendetta
Ch'al fin chi morte
Da la morte aspetta.

A Woman Knows Not What She Says, and Does Not Say What She Knows

Enticing lovers, the affected hope is a poison of hearts.

Oh God, how I understand the feminine habit, women never make a true promise. So it goes, he who hopes for nothing has much more.

The chatting, laughing one with full courtesy answers my prayers.

Oh God, how I understand the feminine lies, women never speak from a truthful mouth. A woman who remains silent says more.

Liar of affection, every pleasure you show at my words.

Oh God, how I understand the feminine graces, women never have staunch faith. So it goes, one enjoys more who believes less.

Denial

If I swear to you upon my life that I love you, immediately with harsh words you contradict me.

I, whose senses are so alive, run to relieve the affront with kisses.

Beautiful Eyes

You wound me, oh beautiful eyes.

Just imagine what these fiery and pungent kisses do: the soul languishes and the heart fails. Oh that my heart dies for you.

Just imagine what these sharp and killing arrows do: the soul languishes and the heart fails. Oh that my heart dies for you.

But perhaps I will not die without revenge, for in the end he who gives death waits for death.

10. Cor donato, cor rubato

A Heart Given, a Heart Stolen

Dori

Tu mendace, tu infedel, no, no
Ch'in don, l'hebbe, no'l rubò
Mi donasti il cor, si, si.
Ben è giusto il rancor aspre,
Aspre le offese
Me 'l donò.

You false one, you unfaithful one, no, no; I had it as a gift, I didn't steal it; you gave me your heart, yes, yes. The bitter rancor, the offenses are right and just. You gave it to me.

Filindo

Ladra, tu ladra crudel,
Mi rubasti il cor, si, si,
Con begl' occhi lo rapi;
Mi rubasti il cor, si, si.
Ben è giusto il rancor aspre,
Aspre le offese.
Me 'l rubò.

Thief, you cruel thief, you stole my heart, yes, yes, with beautiful eyes you kidnapped it; you stole my heart, yes, yes. The bitter rancor, the offenses are right and just. You stole it from me.

Tirsi

Fermate; lasciate, le contese.
Tropp'è ingiusto il rancor false le offese.
Miracol fu d'amore,
Cessi l'ingiusta lite.
No 'l donò, no 'l rubbò.
Fermate, udite.

Stop the arguments. The rancor is too unjust and the offenses false. It was a miracle of love; let the unjust dispute cease. You [Filando] didn't give it, you [Dori] didn't steal it. Stop, listen.

Amor, amor che tutto puote un cuore
Un' alma toglie da un seno
E' in altro sen l'innesta,
Se spira humana
Salma priva del core.
Opra in amore è questa.

Love can do anything to a heart; it can take the soul from one heart and place it in another. If a human body dies without the heart, it is the labor of love.

Dori

No 'l donò, no 'l rapi,
Opra e' d'amor, si, si.
Vivi tu nel mio seno
Vivo, si, nel tuo seno.
Tal morendo beato
Puoi riamando amato,
Rigoder nella tomba
Il di sereno.

You didn't give it, I didn't kidnap it; it is the labor of love, yes, yes. You live in my heart, I live in your heart. Thus dying happy, one can love and be loved in return, and enjoy again the peaceful day in the tomb.

Filindo

No 'l donò, no 'l rapi,
Opra e' d'amor, si, si.
Vivo, si, nel tuo seno
Vivi tu nel mio seno.
Tal morte beata
Puoi riamando amata,
Rigoder nella tomba
Il di sereno.

I didn't give it, you didn't kidnap it; it is the labor of love, yes, yes. I live in your heart, you live in my heart. Thus dying happy, one can love and be loved in return, and enjoy again the peaceful day in the tomb.

Tirsi

No 'l donò, no 'l rapi,
Opra è d'amor, si, si.
Spira tu co 'l suo core,
Vivi tu nel suo seno,
Vivi, si, si, nel suo seno.
Tal morendo beato

Dori, Filindo, Tirsi

Puoi riamando amato
Rigoder nella tomba
Il di sereno.

You [Filando] didn't give it, you [Dori] didn't kidnap it; it is the labor of love, yes, yes. You die with his heart; you live, yes, in her breast. Thus you die happy.

Thus dying happy, one can love and be loved in return, and enjoy again the peaceful day in the tomb.

11. Desideri vani

Desideri che?
Desideri che sperate di gioir.
Voi v'ingannate.

Può ben grand' ale
Ingigantito il core
Spiegar al ciel d'amore,
Mentre dalla crudel
Che vi fa guerra
Vostre speranze in terra
Piombano fulminate.

In vano ergete
Ardimentoso il guardo
Ad un seren bugiardo,
Mentr'al vostro salir
Fiere procelle
Dalle nemiche stelle
Vengono minacciate.

Desideri che?
Desideri che sperate di gioir.
Voi v'ingannate..

Vain Desires

What desires? Desires that you hope will bring joy. You deceive yourself.

The heart, blossoming, can spread its enormous wings in the sky of love; while because of the cruel one who makes war against you, your hopes rain suddenly to the earth.

In vain you lift your proud gaze to a contented liar, while at your rising the powerful storm from the starry enemies comes to threaten.

What desires? Desires that you hope will bring joy. You deceive yourself.

CANTATE

ARIETE A VNA, DVE, E TRE VOCI

OPERA TERZA

DI

BARBARA STROZZI

NOVAMENTE STAMPATE

STAMPA DEL GARDANO

IN VENETIA DC LIIII *Appresso Francesco Magni*

Plate 1. Barbara Strozzi, *Cantate, Ariete a una, due, e tre voci, opera terza* (Venice: Gardano, 1654), title page (courtesy of British Library, London)

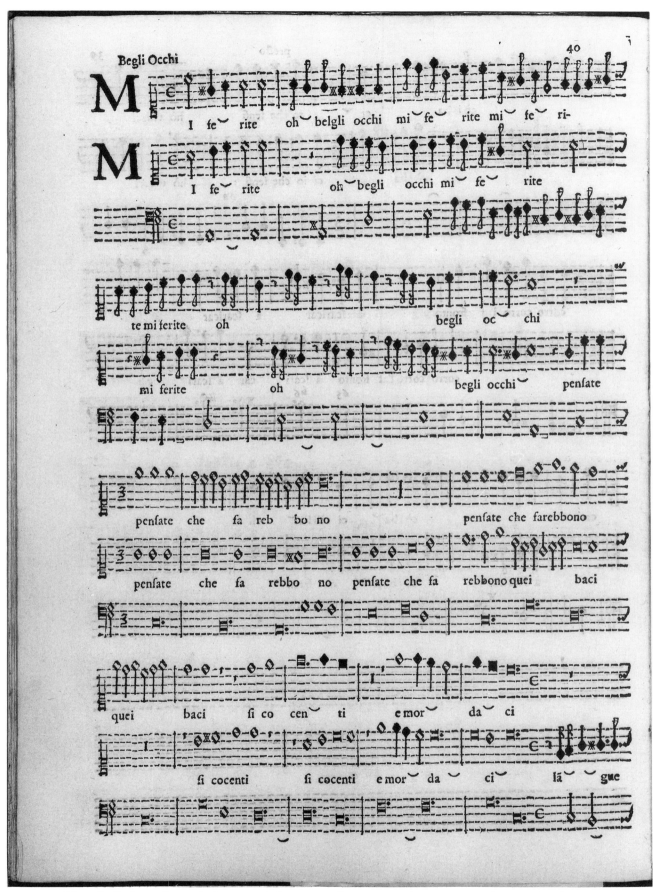

Plate 2. Barbara Strozzi, *Cantate, Ariete a una, due, e tre voci, opera terza* (Venice: Gardano, 1654), opening of "Begli occhi," page 40 (courtesy of British Library, London)

CANTATE, ARIETE A UNA, DUE, E TRE VOCI

1. Cuore che reprime alle lingua
di manifestare il nome della sua cara

Seconda parte

Terza & Ultima parte

Qual sia l'as- - pro, l'as- - pro mio sta- to, Qual sia l'as- pro mio _____

sta- to _____ Ri- dir nol pon- no i ven- -

- - ti, Nep- pur le sel- ve o l'on-de, Nep- pur le sel- ve o' l'on- de u-di-

-ro i miei la- men- - - -

- ti, Ma so- lo il duol en- tro al mio cor, _____ en- tro al mio cor _____

_____ s'as- con- - -

-co a po- co a po- co a po- co

E s'ad al- tri la lin- gua, la lin- gua È scor-ta al- la lor _ sor- te, la lin- gua È scor-ta al- la lor _

sor- te, A me la lin- gua è sol ca- gion di mor- te, __

A me la lin- gua, a me la lin- gua è sol ca-

-gion di mor- te. __

2. Moralità amorosa

Seconda parte

a- di- tar al- trui co- me s'a- do- ri.

Po- scia con sot- ti- lis- si- mi can- do-

-ri Spar- - ge, spar- - ge del l'au- reo

ca- po o- - gni con- fi- ne,

Che di pol- ve di ci- pri ar- gen- te e bri- ne

Fan- no of- fi- cio di smal- to, fan- no of- fi- cio di smal-

"Sei fret- to- lo- so an- da- to A di-chia-rar un per- fi-do, un fel- lo- ne, Quel ser-vo a te si gra- to? Men- tre, men- tre, Fran- ze- se Au- gus- to, Di me- ri- tar pro- -cu- ri il ti- to- lo, il ti- to- lo di Gius- to? Tu, se' l mio fal- lo di gas- ti- go è de- gno, Ohi- mè, ch'in-sie-me in- sie- me Del-l'in-vi- dia che fre- me Vit- ti- ma, del-l'in-vi- dia che fre- me vit- ti- ma mi sa-cri- fi- chi al- lo sde- gno. Non mi chia- mo in-no- cen- te: Pur-trop-po er-rai pur- trop- po Ho me

stes- so tra- di- to A cre- der al- l'in- vi- to___ di for- tu- na___

ri- den- te. Non mi chia- mo in- no- cen-

-te: ___ Gran- d'au- ra di fa-

-vo- ri Rea la me- mo- ria___ fe- ce___ Di co- sì stol- - ti___ er-

-ro- ri, Un nem- bo del- l'ob- bli- o Fu la ca- gion del pre- ci- pi- zi- o

mi- o,___ Fu la ca- gion del pre- ci- pi- zi- o mi- o.___ Ma che di-

-c'io? Tu, Si- re,— ah, chi nol ve- de?— Tu sol, cre-den-do trop-po al- la mia fe- de, M'hai

fat- to in re- gia cor- te Ber- sa-glio del-l'in-vi- di-a e reo, e reo di___ mor- te.___

Ritornello adagio

Men- tre al de- vo- to, al de-vo- to

col- lo Tu mi sten-de- vi quel cor- te- se, quel cor- te- se, cor- te- se, cor- te-

- se brac- cio, Al- lor mi da- vi, al- lor mi da-vi il crol-lo, Al- lor, al- lor tu m'ap-pres-

133
-vea, do- vea pur dir- mi, oh___ Di- o, oh___ Di- o, Mia for- tu- na in- co- stan- te.___

136

140
Quan-do me- co gio- i- vi Di se-guir cer-vo fug-gi- ti-

143
- vo, al- lo- ra L'a- ni- mal in- no-cen-te Dai ca- ni la-ce-ra-to Fi- gu-

146
-ra- va il mio sta- to, Es-pos-to ai mor- si di ac-ca- ni- ta gen- te. ___ Non con-dan- no il mio

150
re, no, no, d'al-tro er- ro- re Che di so- ver- chio a- mo- re,___

6

154
_ no, no, d'al- tro er- ro- re che di so- ver- chio, di so-

158
-ver- chio a- mo- re. _____ Di cin- que mar- che il-

162
-lus- tre No- ta- to e- ra il mio no- me, Ma de- gli e- mo- li miei l'in- si- die in-

166
-dus- tri Han- no di tra- di- tri- ce al- la mia tes- ta Da- ta la mar- ca ses- ta.

171
Ha l'in- vi- dia vo- lu- to Che, se col- pe- vol so- no, Es- clu- so dal per-

175
-do- no Es- tin- to an- co- ra, ⟨an- co- ra⟩ im- man- ti- nen- te io ca- da; Col mio san- gue ha sa-

179
-pu- to De' suoi tri- on- fi im- por- po- rar la _____ stra- da.

184
Nel- la gra- zia del __ mio __ re men-tr'in su trop- po men vo,

188
Di ve- nir __ die- tro al mio __ piè _____ La for- tu- na si __ stan-

192
-cò, la for- tu- na si stan- cò. _____

196
_ On- de ho pro- va- to, ahi _____ las-

200
-so, Co- me dal tut- to al nien- te è un bre- ve pas- so." _

204

Lu- i- gi, a ques-te no- te Di vo- ce che per- don sup- pli- ce chie- de,

208

Ti- mo- ro- so, ti- mo- ro- so si ____ scuo- te

211

E del mor- to gar- zon la fac- cia ____ ve- de.

215

Men- tre il re col suo pian- to Del- le sue fret- te il

218

pen- ti- men- to ac-cen- na Tre- mò Pa- ri- gi, tre-mò Pa-

221

-ri- gi e tor- bi- dos- si, tor- bi- dos- si Sen- na. ____

4. A donna bella e crudele

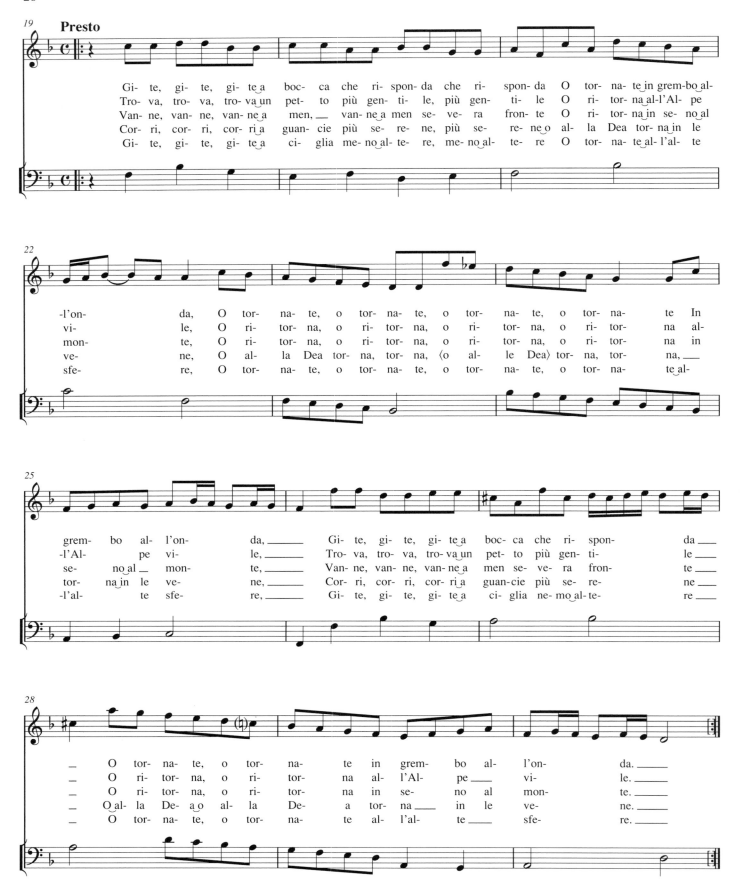

5. Con male nuove, non si può cantare

6. Amor non si fugge

[1, 3, 5] Ca- ra, ca- ra fil- li, quel- la tu se- i, tu sei,
quel- la ____ ch'a- do- ro, Per te so- la, per te, per te
so- la, per te lan- gui- sco e mo- ro.

[Fine]

[2] Ben vi- d'io ch'un ____ guar- do a- des- ca Ch'al- let- tan- do il
[4] S'e il lan- guir ____ col- po ____ d'a- mo- re Fug- gi- rò ____ s'a-

se- ____ no a- dug- ge, Ma ____ pur ar-
-mor _____ m'as- sa- le, Ma 'l fug- gir, ____

[D.C. al Fine]

7. Donna non sà che dice, non dice che sà

Soprano
Lu- sin- ghie- ra, lu- sin- ghie- ra, lu- sin- ghie- ra d'a- mo- ri

Bass
Lu- sin- ghie- ra, lu- sin- ghie- ra, lu- sin- ghie- ra d'a- mo- ri La vez-

Continuo

La vez- zo- sa spe- ran- za, La vez- zo-

-zo- sa spe- ran- za, la vez- zo- sa,

- sa spe- ran- za È un ve- le-

La vez- zo- sa spe- ran- za È un ve- le- no, ve- le- no, ve-

- no dei co- ri. Lu- sin- ghie- ra, lu- sin- ghie- ra,

-le- no dei co- ri. Lu- sin- ghie- ra, lu- sin- ghie- ra, lu- sin-

-mes- sa, pro- mes- sa ve- ra, Non è di don- na mai Pro- mes- sa, pro- mes- sa ve- ra. _

ve- ra, Non è di don- na mai, Non è di don- na mai Pro- mes- sa, pro- mes- sa ve-

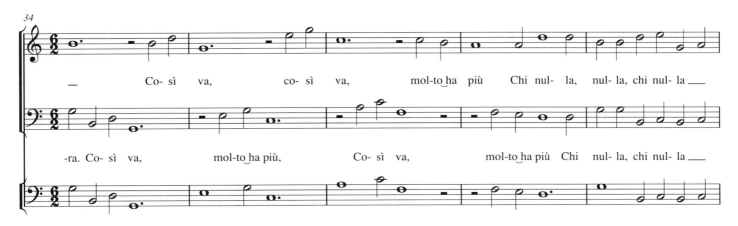

_ Co- sì va, co- sì va, mol- to ha più Chi nul- la, nul- la, chi nul- la _

-ra. Co- sì va, mol- to ha più, Co- sì va, mol- to ha più Chi nul- la, chi nul- la ___

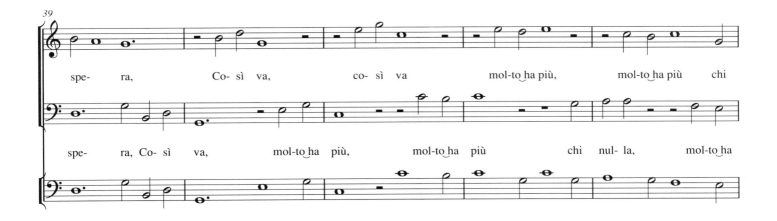

spe- ra, Co- sì va, co- sì va mol- to ha più, mol- to ha più chi

spe- ra, Co- sì va, mol- to ha più, mol- to ha più chi nul- la, mol- to ha

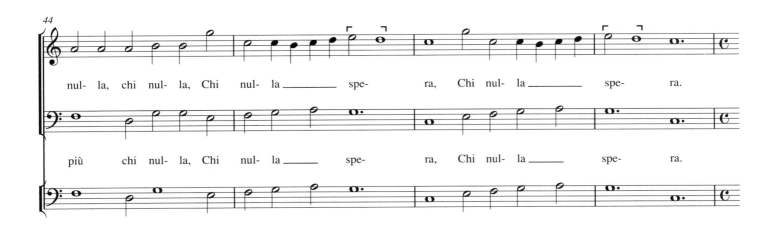

nul- la, chi nul- la, Chi nul- la _ spe- ra, Chi nul- la _ spe- ra.

più chi nul- la, Chi nul- la _ spe- ra, Chi nul- la _ spe- ra.

8. Mentita

Su- bi- to u- na men- ti- ta, u- na men- ti-

Su- bi- to u- na men- ti- ta, men - ti- ta, __

-ta, con pa-ro- le spie- ta- te Su- bi- to, su - bi- to u- na men-

__ con pa-ro- le spie-ta- te su- bi- to, con pa-ro- le spie-ta- te Su- bi- to

-ti- ta, men-ti- ta. S'io vi giu- ro, vi giu- ro Ch'io v'a- mo, mia vi- ta Ch'io v'a- mo, mia

u- na men-ti- ta. S'io vi giu- ro, vi giu- ro Ch'io v'a- mo, mia vi- ta Ch'io v'a- mo, mia

vi- ta Voi, voi, voi mi da- te, mi da- te Su- bi- to u-

vi- ta, Voi, voi, voi mi da- te, mi da- te, voi, voi, voi mi da- te u- na,

9. Begli occhi

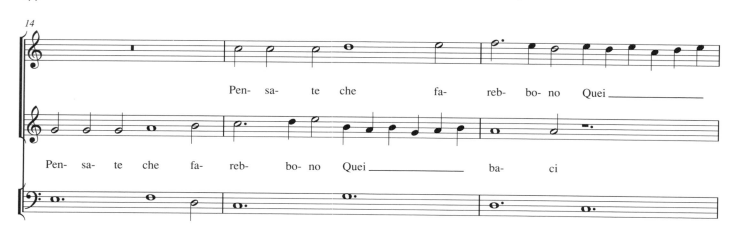

Pen- sa- te che fa- reb- bo- no Quei _____

Pen- sa- te che fa- reb- bo- no Quei _____ ba- ci

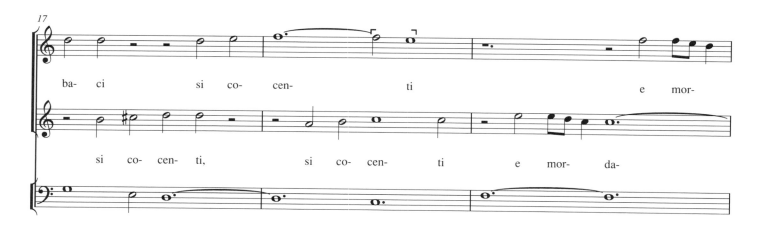

ba- ci si co- cen- ti e mor-

si co- cen- ti, si co- cen- ti e mor- da-

-da- ci; Lan- gue l'a- ni- ma,

- ci; _____ Lan- gue l'a- ni- ma, lan- gue,

lan- gue, E il _____ cor vien _____ me- no, E il _____ cor vien _____

E il _____ cor, e il _____ cor vien _____ me- no, E il _____ cor vien _____

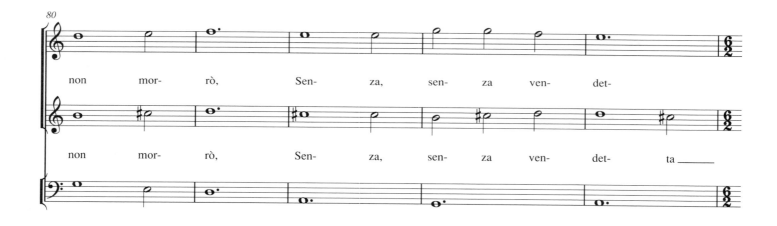

-pet- ta, Ch'al fin chi mor- te Da la mor- te, la

mor- te _____ Da la mor- te as- pet- ta, la mor- te, la

mor- te as- -

mor- te as-

- - pet- ta.

- - pet- ta. _____

10. Cor donato, cor rubato

Contrasto tra Filindo, Dori e Tirsi

52

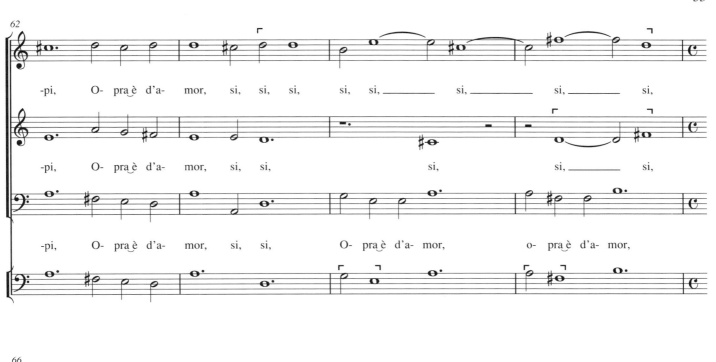

tu,   Vi-   vo, si,   si,   nel tuo se-   no.

vi- vo, si, Vi- vi tu nel mio se- no,   Vi- vi tu nel mio se-   no.

Vi- vi, si,   si,   si,   vi- vi, si, nel suo se-   no.

Tal,   tal   mo- ren- do be- a-   to

Tal,   tal mor- te be- a-   ta   Puoi ri- a-

Tal,   tal   mo- ren- do be- a-   to

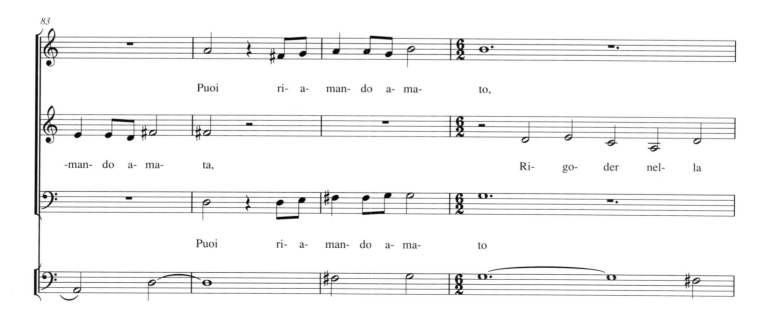

Puoi ri- a- man- do a-ma-   to,

-man- do a-ma-   ta,   Ri- go- der nel- la

Puoi ri- a- man- do a-ma-   to

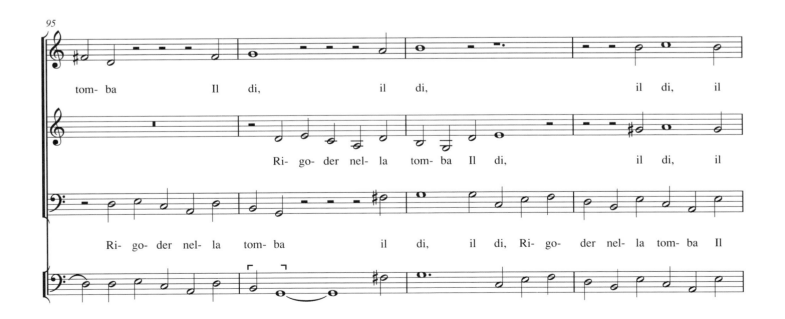

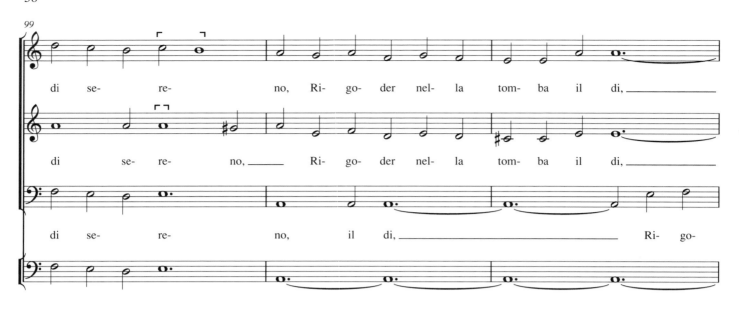

di se- re- no, Ri- go- der nel- la tom- ba il di, _____

di se- re- no, _____ Ri- go- der nel- la tom- ba il di, _____

di se- re- no, il di, _____ Ri- go-

_____ il di, Il di _____ se- re- no.

_____ il di, Il di _____ se- re- no. _____

-der nel- la tom- ba il di, il di, Il di se- re- no.

11. Desideri vani

64

Critical Report

Editorial Method

Strozzi's *Cantate, ariete a una, due, e tre voci*, opus 3, survives in a single volume published by Gardano in Venice in 1654 (RISM S6985), held by the British Library, London, shelf number K.7.g.4.(1.). This print is the principal source for the edition and the only known complete source. The five solo works of the opus 3 collection, plus the opus 2 version of *Il lamento*, appear in facsimile in *Cantatas by Barbara Strozzi*, edited by Ellen Rosand, in The Italian Cantata in the Seventeenth Century, vol. 5 (New York: Garland, 1986).

The seventh cantata, *Donna non sà che dice, non dice che sà*, provided the model for the editorial method used in preparing the edition. The basic unit of the compound meter indicated by the numeral **3** in this cantata is the dotted semibreve, or whole note in modern notation. A modern signature of $\frac{6}{2}$ is applied to these sections, and regular barring has been added to the inconsistent barring of the original, and a $\frac{3}{2}$ bar is sometimes necessary at the close of a section. When the triple sections of the print use the dotted breve as the metric unit, the note values have been halved, and this is reported in the critical notes; $\frac{3}{2}$ sections in the original have been retained. Coloration is used for hemiola effects and is marked in the score by open horizontal brackets. The one instance in which **3** clearly indicates the minim (dotted half note) is in the arietta, *Amor non si fugge*. Here the original values are retained and regular barring added. All duple sections appear as in the print except for the added bar lines that are placed at the interval of the semibreve. Throughout the transcription, the modern whole note is substituted for tied half notes within a single measure of common time.

Modern clefs are substituted for the various C clefs of the vocal parts. The original accidentals are retained and repeated in succeeding measures according to modern practice. Cautionary accidentals that do not appear in the print are given in parentheses in the edition. Other editorial accidentals are given in square brackets. In the print, Gardano raises a flat with a sharp and lowers a sharp with a flat. This has been modernized in the edition; for example, the note B-sharp in a section with a signature of one flat in the print is given as B-natural in the edition.

Neither capitalization nor punctuation are consistent in the text underlay of the print. Both have been made consistent by the editor according to the structure of the Italian poetry. Spelling, including the use of accents, has been modernized. Text repetitions indicated by the rubric *"ij"* in the print have been realized in the edition within angle brackets. In most cases the number of syllables coincides with the available notes. When this is not the case, strong syllables are applied to strong beats, and the remainder are adjusted to fit. Problems arise with the large number of syllables crowded into the limited space of the *presto* section of *A donna bella e crudele*; the smaller, discreet type of the modern edition permits the splitting of words into syllables ("men se-ve-ra," verse 3, m. 27) and adjusting each verse to correspond one to the other. Slurs marking melismas and text underlay have been eliminated in favor of hyphens and word extensions.

Critical Notes

The original print is virtually error free in pitch and rhythmic notation. (See above for discussion of meter, barring, and clefs.) References to vocal parts are abbreviated as follows: S = soprano; A = mezzo-soprano; B = basso; and B.c. = continuo. Pitches are given according to the system in which middle C = c'.

1. *Cuore che reprime alle lingua di manifestare il nome della sua cara*

Mm. 31–44, note values halved. Mm. 52–62, note values halved. Mm. 85–98, note values halved. Mm. 103–21, note values halved.

3. *Il lamento*

Mm. 100–139, note values halved. M. 177, *ij.* for "ancora" follows "immantinente."

5. *Con male nuove, non si può cantare*

M. 40, S, B.c., note 3 is a whole note.

7. *Donna non sà che dice, non dice che sà*

M. 98, S, B, B.c., note 1 is a whole note; B.c., note 1 is E. Mm. 102–9, note values halved.

8. *Mentita*

Mm. 15–17, note values halved. Mm. 22–32, note values halved.

9. *Begli occhi*

Mm. 12–20, note values halved. Mm. 38–44, note values halved. Mm. 74–78, note values halved. M. 85, B.c., note 1 is a dotted whole note, note 3 is a whole note. Mm. 85–90, note values halved.

10. *Cor donato, cor rubato*

Mm. 68–77, note values halved.

11. *Desideri vani*

M. 39, S, note 6, e♭". M. 44, A, note 3, e♭'.

WOMEN COMPOSERS

Amy Beach
QUARTET FOR STRINGS (IN ONE MOVEMENT) OPUS 89
Edited by Adrienne Fried Block
Recognized as America's leading woman composer in the late nineteenth and early twentieth centuries, Amy Beach (1867–1944) belonged to the Second New England School of composers. Her one-movement quartet, a lean yet lyrical work of great originality, incorporates Alaskan Inuit melodies as thematic material. Completed in 1929, the quartet was one of Beach's few unpublished works. This edition, which includes a facsimile of the 1921 draft score, makes the work available for the first time.
A 23/MUSA 3 (1994)—$43.20; parts—$20.00/set
ISBN 0-89579-291-5

Ruth Crawford
MUSIC FOR SMALL ORCHESTRA (1926)
SUITE NO. 2 FOR FOUR STRINGS AND PIANO (1929)
Edited by Judith Tick and Wayne Schneider
By the late 1920s, before composing her landmark String Quartet 1931, Ruth Crawford (1901–53) had already found a strong and individual voice as an American modernist. This edition presents two important unpublished compositions from that period: Music for Small Orchestra (1926) and Suite No. 2 for Four Strings and Piano (1929). The style of these works, dubbed "post tonal pluralism," shows Crawford handling tonality as an option rather than a premise as she responds originally to a range of musical, literary, and intellectual currents.
A 19/MUSA 1 (1993); second edition(1996)—$43.20;
Music for Small Orchestra parts—$22.00/set;
Suite No. 2 parts —$14.00/set
ISBN 0-89579-326-1

Fanny Hensel
SONGS FOR PIANOFORTE, 1836–1837
Edited by Camilla Cai
These piano pieces were composed by Fanny Hensel (1805–47) when she was in her early thirties, and she planned to publish ten of these eleven pieces as a unified set. Only one of the eleven pieces was published during Hensel's lifetime. The remaining ten, based on the autograph manuscripts, are published here for the first time.

Contents
No. 1 Allegretto grazioso; No. 2 Andante; No. 3 Prestissimo; No. 4 Allegro con brio; No. 5 Allegro con spirito; No. 6 Allegro con brio; No. 7 Allegro agitato; No. 8 Allegro moderato; No. 9 Largo con espressione; No. 10 Capriccio: Allegro ma no troppo; [Unnumbered] Allegro agitato; No. 1 Allegro vivace (Version 1)

N 22 (1994)—$38.40
ISBN 0-89579-293-1

Isabella Leonarda
SELECTED COMPOSITIONS
Edited by Stewart Carter
Although Isabella Leonarda (1620–1704) wrote more music than any other woman of the Baroque era, only one of her nearly 200 extant compositions has previously appeared in a modern edition. This volume reveals Leonarda's highly expressive style and offers a representative sampling of her works in various genres. Included are two concerted liturgical works (a Kyrie and a psalm setting), four motets, and two sonatas.

Contents
Sacred Vocal Compositions with Liturgical Texts
Kyrie, from Messa concertata, Op. 4, No. 1; Beatus vir, Op. 19, No. 4
Sacred Vocal Compositions with Extra-liturgical Texts
Volo Jesu, Op. 3, No. 6; Care plage, cari ardores, Op. 17, No. 9; Ad arma, o spiritus, Op. 13, No. 3; Paremus nos, fideles, Op. 13, No. 11
Instrumental Compositions
Sonata Prima, Op. 16, No. 1; Sonata duodecima, Op. 16, No. 12

B 59 (1988)—$38.40; performance parts available
ISBN 0-89579-227-3

Maddalena Laura Sirmen
THREE VIOLIN CONCERTOS
Edited by Jane L. Berdes
Maddalena Laura Sirmen (1745–1818) was the single renowned product of those Venetian conservatories devoted exclusively to educating women as musicians to have become internationally famous as a composer. All of the pieces were published widely in England, France, and the Netherlands—some in as many as five editions. The Violin Concertos are rare examples of the mature classical style in Venice during the late 1760s.

Contents
Concerto I in B-flat Major; Concerto III in A Major; Concerto V in B-flat Major
Appendix: Cadenzas by Robert E. Seletsky

C 38 (1991)—$38.40; performance parts available
ISBN 0-89579-262-1

Send or Fax orders to:

A-R Editions, Inc.
801 Deming Way
Madison, WI 53717
800-736-0070
608-831-8200 (fax)
http://www.areditions.com